The Star/Cross
An Entrance Meditation

Books by Ira Progoff

The Practice of Process Meditation:
The *Intensive Journal* Way to Spiritual Experience, 1980

At a Journal Workshop: The Basic Text and Guide
for Using the *Intensive Journal* Process, 1975

The Symbolic and the Real, 1963

Depth Psychology and Modern Man, 1959

The Death and Rebirth of Psychology, 1956

The Cloud of Unknowing, 1957

The Image of an Oracle, 1964

Jung's Psychology and Its Social Meaning, 1953

Jung, Synchronicity and Human Destiny, 1973

The Star/Cross, 1971

The White Robed Monk, 1972, 1979, 1981

The Well and the Cathedral, 1971, 1977, 1981

The Star/Cross
An Entrance Meditation

Ira Progoff

DIALOGUE HOUSE LIBRARY/NEW YORK

Published by Dialogue House Library
80 East 11 Street, New York, New York 10003
Copyright © 1971, 1972, 1981 by Ira Progoff
First Printing, 1971
Second Printing, 1972
Third Printing, 1976
Second Enlarged Edition, 1981

LC-70-17611   Paperback ISBN 0-87941-001-09

Printed in the United States of America

Table of Contents

THE ENTRANCE MEDITATION SERIES

The Well and the Cathedral
The Star/Cross
The White Robed Monk

Preface

to the

Entrance

Meditation

Series

The meditations in this series have evolved in the course of a decade of use in public workshops, in religious services, in university teaching and in therapeutic work. Their purpose is to provide a means of *entering* the realm of quiet and depth where interior knowing takes place.

Where a person's spiritual life is concerned, we know that the door opens inward. It is through this door that we gain access to the elusive range of awarenesses where we find the meaning of our lives. Entrance Meditation enables us to go to that place within ourselves from which we can reach beyond ourselves. This is its purpose. Once Entrance Meditation has taken us through the entry way, it leaves us free to follow our own rhythms of inner experience and to move in whatever direction to explore whatever doctrines feel right to us.

Some of us may then embark on a great voyage of inward exploration and discovery, finding new realities we never perceived before. Others of us will remain within traditions and beliefs that we have always known, but our Entrance Meditation experience will so deepen our perception of their meaning that we will feel we have just discovered an altogether new truth. There are many paths that can be followed once we are within the realm of spiritual experience. We have true inner religious freedom there. The purpose of these meditations is to enable us to enter that realm. Our entrance meditations thus become the base and neutral starting point for all the further spiritual recognitions that may come to us. By providing a non-doctrinal means of gaining access to our inner space, they enable us to perceive and judge for ourselves the quality and the reality of the spiritual dimension of experience.

The conception of entrance meditation was originally developed within the framework of the *Intensive Journal* program. Over the years the meditations included in this series have had their largest use as aids for deepening personal experience within the context of *Intensive Journal* workshops. But the use of these entrance meditations is by no means limited to *Intensive Journal* work. They have been used independently by ministers conducting meditative services, by philosophy professors seeking to take their students to the inner place where they can share the experiences of the great philosophers of history, and by therapists of various types seeking to establish a depth atmosphere for their patients or clients.

The reports that have been brought to me regarding these experiences indicate that the use of entrance meditation is especially valuable in situations where a deepening of atmosphere facilitates the work that has been undertaken, whatever the purposes or beliefs of that work may be. One important reason it is able to do this is that these meditations tend to establish an atmosphere by means of symbols that are altogether neutral. These symbols are not tied to any specific system of doctrine or belief, and yet they express fundamental truths of human existence. They provide a vehicle, a means of entering the deep realms of reality in human experience. Thus they can serve in a neutral, non-dogmatic fashion as a way inward. And each person can reach by means of them a contact with truth in the terms of his or her own traditions and consciousness.

These meditations arose from experiences that came to me over a period of time in the course of my personal work in the *Intensive Journal* process, and especially in my personal practice of Process Meditation. Originally they were intended merely to give expression to my personal experiences. As I used them in *Intensive Journal* workshops, however, and then as others used them in their own frameworks wherever a deepened atmosphere might be helpful, we found that these experiences served a more-than-personal use. With this thought in mind they have been worked with experimentally over the years, and published in various editions on a trial and error basis in search of the format in which they can best serve.

The present edition of the Entrance Meditation Series is the result of this decade-long process of experimentation. It now contains *The Well and the Cathedral,* *The White Robed Monk,* and *The Star/ Cross* in a unified format, each moving through a cycle of eight units of meditative experience. Each unit is self-contained so that it can be used individually but the eight units in each of the volumes move in sequence developing their theme through a full cycle of experiences. When you work with these entrance meditation books, you may find that you prefer to work with each volume as a whole. Or you may find that you prefer to choose particular sections of the individual volumes and concentrate on them, using them to deepen and open your own experience. Work experimentally with them until you find the way that is spiritually most valuable for you.

Of the three volumes in this series *The Well and the Cathedral* expresses in the most fundamental form the principles that underlie the cycles of meditative experience. It contains a minimum of symbols, and these are mainly metaphors chosen for their functional use in helping a person move inward. The symbols serve as vehicles by which we can enter the depth levels of experience. They take you immediately into the practice of entrance meditation so that you can know it directly by experiencing it. And you experience it by participating in its practice.

In order to begin, there is little need to elaborate the principles and methods of entrance meditation. Essentially you can begin to use these meditations in the same way that a fish learns to swim: it finds itself in the water and it does what comes naturally. In the same natural way you can move directly into your meditative experience starting with any one of the volumes in this series. After your work in the quiet way of entrance meditation has established a deep atmosphere in which you can move about comfortably, you may wish to continue with the active procedures of Process Meditation. But that is a further step and an option before you.*

As you work with *The Well and the Cathedral* you will perceive that its neutral symbols take you inward, and then draw you back up to the surface of

* For the principles and techniques of Process Meditation see Ira Progoff, *The Practice of Process Meditation,* Dialogue House Library, N.Y. 1980. This is a companion volume to Ira Progoff, *At a Journal Workshop,* the basic guide and text of the *Intensive Journal* process (1975 cloth, 1977 paperback).

life. It is a cyclical movement. But it is also progressive because each phase of the cycle tends to take you deeper than the one before. There is thus a cumulative, deepening effect that establishes itself as you continue with the sequence of units of *The Well and the Cathedral.* But nothing of what takes place determines or even suggests what your experiences will be or what aspects of truth you will recognize. It merely gives you a progressive means of entering the depth dimension of your inner life.

There are many theories that deal with this inner realm, seeking to tell us what it is and what it contains. Many philosophies in the course of history have spoken of its mysteries, claiming to describe what is to be found there, giving a roadmap and instructions, telling seekers how they should behave. Entrance meditation makes no such presumption, but its practice does open another possibility. It enables us actually to enter our own inner space in order that we can find out for ourselves what is there. It does not predetermine what we shall discover. It does not give us rules telling us how we *should* experience it, nor what we shall believe about what we find there. It simply takes us to a progressively deeper place in quietness and then lets us go free, each to perceive a larger dimension of reality in which we may place the meaning of our life.

Each of the sequences of entrance meditation in this series follows the procedure of taking us progressively inward into the depths and then letting us go free to explore. The eight units of *The Well and the Cathedral* express this essence of entrance meditation in an altogether non-doctrinal form. The experiences described there are generic and universal. The experiences described in *The Star/Cross* and *The White Robed Monk* are more specific and individualized. Their symbols tend to set a direction and establish a definite tone for the inner work that is done with them. The experiences of *The White Robed Monk* move in a contemplative direction, invoking the atmosphere that comes with systematic religious practice. They do not presume any specific religious discipline, however. The experiences of *The Star/Cross* draw upon the spirituality of the world of nature, taking us each "into the forest of our life." There we come to the further questions of social justice and the painful events of history, seeking to understand them by the light of inner vision, "the path of the Prophets of old." Each of us may then consider the problems of society and history in our own spiritual perspective.

As we work in them, we must bear in mind that all three sequences of entrance meditation are only starters. They take us inward; and after they have taken us through the doorway into the depth dimension of experience, they give us the freedom to continue on our own. At any given time we may find that the particular cycle of meditation with which we are working is shaping our experiences, perhaps by influencing at a non-conscious level the direction in which we move, perhaps by the suggestive quality of its symbols. Each of us can then choose which cycles of entrance meditation we shall work with most actively. We may find also that there are certain units within the entrance meditations that we feel to be more closely related to our inner condition, more akin to our spiritual needs at the time.

There are a few specific guidelines that will be helpful in working with the entrance meditations in this series.

Our first step is to read a unit of meditation to ourselves, or to hear it read at a meditation workshop or service, or to play it on a cassette. We should continue with it until we come to the cue phrase at the close of the unit, "In the Silence . . . In the Silence." It is best to continue with it through the full reading of the unit, and not to leave it in the middle, not even in order to record a fresh stirring of experience. We wish to allow the cyclical movement of each unit to draw us fully into the stillness. If new experiences stir within us, we can let them accumulate and still remember them, recording them briefly as we come into the silence. In the midst of the meditation we do not think about it nor evaluate it nor interpret it. We simply enter the meditation, become part of it and go with it without seeking to direct or shape it in any way.

While reading or listening to the meditation, we consciously breathe slowly and softly. We do not follow any special or complicated calisthenic of breathing. We simply breathe in our accustomed way as feels natural to us. Now, however, as we are sitting in stillness, we breathe a little more slowly than we ordinarily would. First we establish the rhythm that feels right to us, and then we try to continue it in a regular way, remaining loose and relaxed as we do so.

Sustaining the breathing in a comfortable and steady rhythm is an important step in beginning the process of meditation. As we proceed and become more accustomed to it, we let ourselves go a little slower and a little slower. Bit by bit in our time of quietness, our breathing slows its pace. As it does so, our entire being, our thinking, our feeling, the tempo of our consciousness and our life, slows its pace. It is a time when the muddiness of our existence can settle into stillness and begin to clarify itself.

In working with a text of entrance meditation, it

is best to proceed one unit at a time, allowing ample time for silence after each unit of meditation. Each unit closes with the phrase, "In the Silence . . . In the Silence" and this is the cue for each of us to move into our own silence. Eyes closed, we turn our attention inward. We are looking inward, but we are not looking merely for things that can be seen. We are looking inward for sounds and words, for symbols and intuitions, for direct knowings and sensations of every kind that may come to us when our attention is turned to the large Twilight realm of Self that lies between unconscious sleep and waking consciousness.* In this state we do not seek any particular type of perception. We do not preconceive what our experience is to be, and especially we do not seek to direct it along any predetermined channel.

When we go into our silence and move into the Twilight range of experience, we are truly exploring. We are looking for information and guidance from a quality of consciousness within us that is other than the thoughts of our personal mind. We try to avoid intruding our expectations and ideas as

---

* For a discussion of Twilight Imaging and other related aspects of the *Intensive Journal* method, see Ira Progoff, *At a Journal Workshop*, Chapter 6, pp. 77ff., Dialogue House Library, N.Y., 1975. See also, Progoff, *The Practice of Process Meditation,* Chapters 5-9.

to what our experience "should" or will be. In particular, we try to refrain from intruding our desires or our willful directions as to what we "want" our experience to be. We are trying to draw new awarenesses from the transpersonal wisdom of life that is carried in the depths within us beyond our egos. One purpose of our practice of entrance meditation is to enable us to learn gradually how to do this. We practice letting it come as it comes, while we remain altogether open and receptive.

In the practice of entrance meditation we are observers of whatever is taking place within us as we sit in silence with our eyes closed and our attention turned inward. What we observe may be visual images that we see, words spoken, themes of music that we hear, sensations within our body, direct intuitive knowings. Whatever its form, as we perceive it we take cognizance of it. We do not judge it, but we recognize it. Neutrally, non-judgmentally, we accept its existence. We accept each perception on the Twilight level as it is, as a fact of our inner process and of our observation. We take note of it and we record it without evaluation.

As new experiences and perceptions come to us, it becomes essential that we record the inner events that are taking place. We should allow sufficient time for our free inner movement to build its own atmosphere and momentum. But we should not let so much time pass that we accumulate more perceptions than we can hold in our memory. On the one hand we do not wish to disrupt the flow of our inner experience. On the other hand we know that if we do not record our experiences as they are happening we shall very likely forget them. And then it will be virtually impossible to recall them again. The key lies in maintaining a balance, a rhythm between the inner perception and the outer recording. It is a rhythm to which we gradually become attuned.

<u>The best way to proceed seems to be to learn to go back and forth from the inner to the outer levels, and back inward again.</u>* In time we become accustomed to making quick, brief but adequate, entries. Writing them from the deep place with our eyes only slightly open, these entries will often be only barely legible when we seek to read them back to ourselves. If, however, we return to rewrite them without letting too long a period elapse, the inner events will be fresh enough in our minds so that we can transcribe and enlarge the notes, even with only a few barely legible words to guide us. Afterwards we take as much time as we need to describe in

* See, e.g., *The Well and the Cathedral*, Unit V, The Downward/ Upward Journey.

detail all that has taken place, amplifying the nuances and elaborating any points that may stimulate us further when we read them back weeks or even months in the future.

An important part of this edition is the open space on the pages on the left side of the book. Those empty pages are for your spontaneous Meditation Log entries. We record what takes place within us as we explore and have new experiences on the Twilight level in the course of our entrance meditations. In what we write here we make no interpretations, nor do we elaborate or explain. We simply describe, briefly and directly, the elusive and subjective perceptions, images and emotions that arise in us in the course of our meditations. And then we move on. It is important also that we record the date of each entry. That will be a valuable piece of information for us when we return to the Meditation Log at a later time.

If you are already working with the *Intensive Journal* process you may wish to record your experiences directly in the Meditation Log section of the *Intensive Journal* workbook that you are using. That will save a step. But a number of persons have told me they feel they have benefited greatly by using the Meditation Log pages in the earlier printings of these entrance meditations. They have used the

Meditation Log in these printed volumes as a means of retaining the spontaneous experiences that came to them while they were working with the text, later copying their entries into the larger Meditation Log section in their *Intensive Journal* workbook. There is a particular value in using the Meditation Log pages in this edition to catch and record your experiences as they come to you while you are in the midst of your work. It is apparently an experience that is common to many persons to find that in the course of copying the entries to transfer them from one book to the other a great deal more is stimulated. Additional experiences are evoked. The recording and transcription of our inner experiences thus become an integral part of the progressive extension of consciousness that is the goal of our entrance meditation work.

Those who are already working in the *Intensive Journal* program are familiar with the varied measures available to us for drawing our Meditation Log entries into an expanding spiritual process. They know that in the *Intensive Journal* work the Meditation Log is not merely a passive recording instrument like a diary; it serves an active, energy-building function. After collecting the raw materials of our inner lives, the Meditation Log selectively feeds the data into the appropriate sections of the

Intensive Journal workbook. Here this material combines with other relevant images and thoughts recorded in other sections and together they may move through a varied combination of exercises. All of these are active exercises, evocation of both psyche and spirit, that build energy and movement as they generate new inner experiences. In the course of these exercises and experiences a person's varied beliefs and religious concerns, intimations and wonderings about meaning in life, are often stimulated and extended into a progressive, open-minded reaching toward truth.

In this phase of the work we are finally able to draw upon the full range of possibilities that the *Intensive Journal* method makes available to us. After using the basic *Intensive Journal* techniques to set the perspective of our life history and to clarify our personal relationships, we can proceed to the more-than-personal issues, the large spiritual agenda of Process Meditation. It is this further phase of the meditative discipline that enables us to expand our spiritual awareness with inner experiences that are directly related to the actualities, the goals and meanings, of our everyday life.*

* For the various ways of working with the Meditation Log section in the *Intensive Journal* workbook, see, in particular, *The Practice of Process Meditation,* Chapters 5, 6, 7, 8, 17, 18.

This is the point of transition in our meditative work. Here we take the important step from the fundamental introductory exercises of entrance meditation to the broad range of explorations and ongoing spiritual involvements that open to us with the practice of Process Meditation. By means of our entrance meditation experiences we can enter the dimension of spiritual reality where inner experiences and transpersonal awareness can come to us. We record these in our Meditation Log. These collected entries then become the raw spiritual data that serve as base points from which we launch our active inner explorations using the Process Meditation techniques within the *Intensive Journal* method. It is a continuous, progressive, and deepening work.

As we prepare now to work with a text of entrance meditation, let us review the steps that we shall follow.

We begin by sitting in stillness, then breathing in a regular rhythm. Working with the meditation texts, we close our eyes. We let ourselves be drawn into the twilight range of perception. Having gained entry there, we observe everything that presents itself to us. We make no judgments, neither accepting nor rejecting, but we take cognizance of whatever is present. We observe it all, and we record as much as we can in our Meditation Log. As we gather it together, the accumulation of data gradually discloses a direction and a purpose as new thoughts and images take form. We begin to see potentials of truth and new meaning unfolding through our inner experiences. We realize that it is not by directing nor by manipulating ourselves psychologically, but by being open in a disciplined way to the progressive stirrings within ourselves that we come personally into contact with the spiritual nature that is our individual and collective heritage as human beings.

Having said this much, we must understand that meditation in all its phases is a work that demonstrates itself and proves itself only as we actually do it. Therefore let us begin, sitting in stillness. . . .

> Letting the Self become still,
> Letting the breath become slow,
> Letting our thoughts come to rest.

I

Letting the Self
Become Still

Meditation Log   *Date*

1. We are sitting
   In a place of quietness
   Letting the Self become still,
   Letting the breath become slow,
   Letting our thoughts come to rest.

2. Letting the Self become still,
   Energies that were moving about
   Can go inward now,
   Can come to rest
   In the stillness
   Of our quiet being.

3. Breathing becomes quiet now,
   Not breathing
   By the tempo of outer things
   But by an inner tempo,
   Breathing at an inner pace,
   The breath moving in
   And out
   Of itself,
   Carried by its own rhythm
   Adjusting itself
   To itself.

4. Breathing at an inner pace,
   Our thoughts let go
   Of our breathing.
   Breathing at an inner pace,
   The breath is free
   To come and go
   In its own timing.
   The breath is slow
   And regular,
   Moving in and out
   By its inner tempo,
   Carried by its own rhythm,
   Adjusting itself
   To itself.

Meditation Log   *Date*

5. Breathing at an inner pace
    Thoughts become quiet,
    Restless thoughts
    That have been moving about,
    Restless thoughts
    Dissipating their energies
    Can come to rest now,
    Can bring their energies together
    Into one place
    Resting
    On the steady breathing.

6. Excess thoughts drop away.
    We become still.
    Thinking becomes quiet,
    Thoughts fitting together
    And settling into one place
    By themselves
    Without our thinking them.
    Many mixed thoughts
    Become one whole thought
    Contained within itself,
    One whole thought
    In the mind at rest.

Meditation Log

Date

7.   Letting the Self become still,
     Letting our thoughts come to rest,
     Letting our breath become slow.
     Breathing becomes quiet,
     Breathing becomes slow,
     And slower;
     Breathing becomes regular,
     Regular.
     The unevenness
     Of nonessential thoughts
     Drops out of the breathing.
     It becomes
     The breathing of the Self.

Meditation Log   *Date*

8. Breathing at an inner pace,
   The breath moves
   At the center of my Self,
   At the center of my Self
   In regular rhythms.
   My body is quiet,
   Holding its place.
   The breath is moving evenly,
   Inward,
   Outward,
   Evenly
   In its own rhythm.
   The breath moves evenly
   At the center of my body,
   At the center of my Self.

Meditation Log   *Date*

9.   The breath is moving
     At the center of my Self
     In a regular rhythm.
     The breath moves at the center.
     The breath moves at the center
     Breathing at an inner pace.
     As the breath moves at the center,
     Quietly,
     Evenly,
     The Self becomes still
     Like quiet water.

10. The Self becomes still
     Like quiet water.
     In the stillness of the Self,
     In the quiet of the water
     My inward ear hears,
     My inward eye sees
     Signs and words and visions
     Reflected in the quiet waters
     In the stillness of the Self,
     In the Silence . . . In the Silence.

II

In the Presence of the Word

Meditation Log   *Date*

1.　Quiet breathing
　　In the stillness,
　　My eyes closed.
　　Not looking at things,
　　I am free to see
　　With an inner awareness.
　　In the stillness of the Self
　　I move nowhere
　　But I reach beyond boundaries.
　　I perceive
　　By an inner perception.

2.　I find myself in a forest.
　　The trees are tall
　　And very close together.
　　The trees overlap one another,
　　Their leaves intertwining.
　　On the ground
　　There is space for me to walk,
　　But above
　　There is no space
　　For sunlight to come through.
　　I know there is sunlight above
　　But none comes through the trees.
　　It is dark in the forest.

3. Standing in the forest
A stillness around me,
A stillness
Deepening,
Surrounding,
Reverberating around me.
The stillness
Echoes through the trees,
The sound of it
Returns and continues.
It is a stillness
And yet it echoes.

4. I stand in stillness
Not moving at all.
A presence is here
Near me
Yet not touching.
Hovering above
And about me
In the darkness of the forest,
It is an encompassing sound
Enveloping everything.

Meditation Log

Date

5.   This shapeless sound
      Pervades the forest.
      It is a Presence,
      Vast beyond form
      But taking form.
      Taking form
      In a word,
      A strange, archaic word,
      It is spoken
      In a resonant and echoing voice . . .
      Tremendum.
      Tremendum.

6.   The word resounds,
      It echoes over my head,
      Tremendum.
      Tremendum.
      I hear the word again,
      Tremendum.
      It is spoken
      But beyond speech . . .
      Tremendum.
      Tremendum.

Meditation Log   *Date*

7. The vastness of a shapeless sound
    Primeval
    Beyond mankind
    Beyond all works and purposes
    Beyond all beliefs,
    The vastness of a shapeless sound
    Taking form in a word,
    Tremendum.

8. I listen to the word.
    It continues to speak,
    Tremendum.
    One word
    Implying many meanings,
    Tremendum.
    The movement of the sound
    Raises me
    Inwardly,
    I am carried
    As by a soft inner wind
    Letting the word speak on . . .
    And listening.

Meditation Log   *Date*

9. Letting the word speak on . . .
    Tremendum.
    One word is spoken,
    I hear many words,
    Carrying many thoughts,
    Mysteries of life,
    Paradoxes of truth
    Contained within one word.

10. Direct knowing,
    Knowing the oneness of life
    Comes while listening,
    Listening in the silence,
    Listening to the word,
    Letting Tremendum speak on
    Letting the word speak on . . .
    And listening,
    Listening . . .
    In the Silence . . . In the Silence.

III

The Glowing Bush

in the Woods

1. After the time of quiet
    Listening in the silence,
    I walk onward
    Into the darkness,
    Deeper into the forest.

2. Walking,
    I come to a small tree,
    Hardly more than a bush,
    It is growing
    Where no bush could possibly grow,
    And it is glowing
    In the darkness of the forest.

3. I notice that this glowing bush
    Does not grow from the ground.
    It is not rooted in the soil
    But takes shape in mid-air.
    There it is flourishing,
    Flowering
    And fully formed.

Meditation Log   *Date*

4. It is a small dogwood
   Covered with white flowers.
   Its trunk does not touch the ground
   And yet it is firm and strong,
   Its white blossoms aglow
   With a soft brightness.
   The brightness is not in the color
   But comes from a glow
   Within the flowers themselves.

5. I am standing deep in the forest.
   Everywhere around me
   It is dark,
   But where I stand
   There is a soft light
   That comes
   From the glowing bush.

6. The glow enlarges itself
    Reaching out to me
    And drawing me toward it.
    We speak,
    The glowing bush and I,
    Not with words
    But with a quality of being
    That passes between us.
    It is gentle
    And quieting
    And assuring.

7. The glowing bush in the woods
    Is connected to me.
    The glowing bush in the woods
    Is part of me.
    I have met a friend in the forest,
    An unexpected friend
    Who will be with me
    As I continue
    In the forest of my life.

Meditation Log   *Date*

---

8. The glowing bush
    Is present
    And will continue to be present.
    It will come with me
    As I continue in the forest,
    As I move onward
    In the forest of my life.
    It will be with me
    Wherever I can see its glow.

9. The glowing bush in the woods,
    A flower in the darkness,
    A light for inner vision.
    The glowing bush in the woods
    Reflects me to myself
    As I stand before it,
    As I stand before it
    In openness of being,
    Listening and speaking,
    Speaking and listening
    In the Silence . . . In the Silence.

IV

The Star/Cross in

the Forest

Meditation Log   *Date*

1. My eyes are closed
    As I go onward
    Deeper into the darkness,
    Exploring the forest
    Within myself,
    And exploring
    The forest of the world
    In which I live.

2. I have never gone this far
    Into the forest before.
    I do not know my way
    Nor what will take place
    As I venture
    Into the forest of my life.
    I have never trodden
    The path of this life.
    I do not know
    What fortune will befall me
    As I proceed
    In the forest of my life.

3.   The glowing bush is with me.
     I feel its presence
     Casting a soft glow
     On the path before me
     As I explore in the darkness,
     Walking among the trees,
     Not knowing where I am walking,
     Exploring
     In the forest of my life.

4.   Suddenly
     In the midst of the forest
     Something appears before me.
     There, in front of a large tree,
     Is a Star of David,
     Fully formed
     And as wide as the tree,
     It is as high
     As my eyes are high.
     It is of no particular color
     But it is distinct.
     I see it clearly before me.

5. Now I see something more.
   Superimposed upon that Star,
   One line fitting vertically
   From the highest point of the Star
   To its lowest point,
   And the other line going horizontally
   Across the top wide line of the Star,
   There is a Cross.

6. I see a Cross
   Fitted upon a Star of David
   Placed upon it
   And placed within it,
   The two perfectly fitting together.
   Each upon the other
   And within the other.
   Neither one is above or below.
   But both are together as one.

Meditation Log   *Date*

7.   I have never seen this Star/Cross before.
It is new to me
But I seem to know it
From somewhere in the past.
The Star/Cross feels warm to me,
Familiar,
Close to me,
Like friends and family
My heart has always known.

8.   Standing before the Star/Cross
I see an open space within it.
At the point where the vertical
And the horizontal
Intersect,
There is an open space.
It is an opening,
Empty and yet full,
Dark and yet luminous,
Unclear, and yet it seems
An infinite space
Opens beyond it.

Meditation Log   *Date*

9.   I close my eyes
And enter the open space
At the center of the Star/Cross.
Visions come to me,
Hearing,
Feeling,
Knowing,
New awarenesses
Are given to me
As I look with eyes closed
Into the open space
At the center of the Star/Cross.

10.   No words are spoken
But the Star/Cross draws me to it
And encourages me
To enter its open space,
To go deeply into it,
Exploring,
Observing,
Remembering
And making note
Of what I perceive.

Meditation Log   *Date*

11. I stand before the Star/Cross
    Looking into the open center
    Where the lines intersect.
    My inner being enters
    The center of the Star/Cross,
    The place of inward visioning
    And inward knowing.
    I enter and explore
    The open space
    At the center of the Star/Cross
    In the Silence . . . In the Silence.

V

*The Center
of the Star/Cross*

Meditation Log   *Date*

1. I look into the open space
    At the center of the Star/Cross.
    The open space is not empty.
    Visions are there,
    Visions of the past
    And of the future,
    Time reflected
    Past and future
    At the center of the Star/Cross.

2. Many visions are shown to me.
    I see them inwardly.
    Many truths made known to me.
    I recognize them
    From within
    As I look intently
    Through the center of the Star/Cross
    Into the open range of time,
    The past and future
    Reflecting their events to me
    And posing their mysteries.

Meditation Log   *Date*

3. From the center of my Self
    I look into the open space
    At the center of the Star/Cross,
    Into the depth of it.
    What can there be
    At the center of the Star/Cross?

4. Now I see.
    There is a teardrop
    At the center of the Star/Cross,
    A teardrop,
    Small and yet boundless
    Reflecting beyond itself,
    A teardrop in the open space
    At the center of the Star/Cross.

Meditation Log   *Date*

5.　Great sorrow is in that tear,
　　The depth of that tear is great.
　　Centuries of sorrowing
　　Have made it deep
　　With many tears.
　　Centuries of sadness
　　Have filled it
　　With waters of sorrow
　　Drawn from many hearts
　　And many lives.

6.　The centuries of sadness
　　Have purified the teardrop
　　At the center of the Star/Cross.
　　As pain makes things pure,
　　Centuries of sorrowing
　　Have cleansed
　　The selfishness,
　　The vanities of power,
　　The pettiness of persons.
　　Now the tear is pure.
　　It became pure
　　Slowly,
　　Painfully.
　　Now it is clear,
　　Its waters are quiet.

Meditation Log   *Date*

7. One teardrop
   At the center of the Star/Cross,
   The turmoil that has been within it
   Is tranquil now.
   History is at rest
   At the center of the Star/Cross,
   The waters of the teardrop are still.
   I look within it to see
   The past and future
   Reflected
   In the waters of the tear
   At the center of the Star/Cross.

8. Eyes closed
   I look into the teardrop
   At the center of the Star/Cross.
   The past is there
   The future is there
   And especially the present.
   The present opens to me
   And shows
   Possibilities
   I had not known before.

Meditation Log   *Date*

9. I enter
   The open range of time
   In the quiet of the tear
   At the center of the Star/Cross,
   Sitting in stillness
   And moving through time
   In the quiet of the tear
   At the center of the Star/Cross
   In the Silence . . . In the Silence.

VI

The Soldiers and

the People

1. I look into the teardrop
   At the center of the Star/Cross.
   It extends
   And deepens,
   It becomes an abyss of waters.
   The sea of human history
   Is reflected in the teardrop
   At the center of the Star/Cross.
   Events are shown to me
   Of past and future.

2. As I look into it
   The waters of the teardrop
   Become a turbulent ocean.
   The passions and angers
   Of the generations,
   The turmoils of history
   Are reflected in the teardrop.
   I see events
   Of many kinds
   At the center of the Star/Cross.

Meditation Log   *Date*

---

3. Now I see
   Within the teardrop
   Many people embracing one another.
   They are soldiers,
   Their clothes are tattered,
   Their faces worn with fatigue,
   But they are embracing one another
   There in the teardrop.

4. I look deeper
   Into the center of the Star/Cross.
   I see many rifles,
   Laid flat upon the ground.
   I see the rifles withering,
   Withering brown
   Like weeds that have been cut,
   And the tired, grimy soldiers
   Are embracing.

5. The soldiers wear uniforms of many nations,
   Their skins, their faces,
   The shape of their heads
   Are different from one another.
   But the soldiers embrace
   As I see them
   In the midst of the teardrop
   At the center of the Star/Cross.

Meditation Log　　　　　　　　　　*Date*

6. Now the vision is changing.
   The soldiers still embrace,
   More than ever now.
   Their affection is greater,
   Their emotions stronger.
   But they are not soldiers any more.
   They are men and women
   Cleanly dressed,
   Each in the style of their country.
   Their children are around them,
   Children of different colors of skin,
   Different colors of hair,
   Different shapes of face.
   And the soldiers,
   Now no longer soldiers,
   Are embracing,
   Men and women embracing,
   Their children around them embracing
   While the rifles are withering brown
   Upon the ground.

Meditation Log   *Date*

7. I see the people embrace
   I hear the sounds of their joy,
   And then the quiet
   Of their peace.
   Now the teardrop is gone.
   Once again
   There is the open space
   At the center of the Star/Cross.
   I look into it deeply,
   Into the open space
   At the center of the Star/Cross
   In the Silence . . . In the Silence.

VII

In the Circles

of History

Meditation Log   *Date*

1. I continue exploring,
    Moving further
    Into the forest of my life,
    Walking in darkness
    Along paths that are covered
    By a tangle of vines and brush.

2. Presently I reach
    A clearing in the forest
    Where the sun shines through the trees.
    I sit upon a stone
    Letting my Self become still,
    Letting my thoughts come to rest,
    Sitting in silence,
    Waiting.

Meditation Log   *Date*

---

3. Out of the silence
    The Star/Cross appears.
    It is present before me
    In the clearing of the forest.
    My attention is drawn
    To the open space
    At the center of the Star/Cross.
    The teardrop is there,
    I can see into it
    At the center of the Star/Cross.

4. Sitting on the stone
    I look to the sky
    Through the center of the Star/Cross.
    Upward
    The universe seems infinite
    Beyond the treetops.
    Looking downward
    I see on the ground
    A mound of field ants
    Moving back and forth,
    In and out,
    Digging, carrying things,
    Busy in an automatic, repetitive way,
    Doing the work of their world.

5. I look at the ants
    Working endlessly at their chores.
    But I see people,
    People in dark garments
    Going to and fro
    Carrying burdens,
    Burdens endlessly
    In the circles of history.
    My heart fills up as I see them,
    I speak a silent blessing of love
    For their weary bodies,
    For their lives without hope
    Carrying burdens
    Through the plodding centuries.

6. Sitting on the stone in the clearing
    I look downward
    And see the ants of history
    Going to and fro before me.
    I look upward
    And see the Star/Cross.
    A thin ray of sunlight
    Is passing through
    The teardrop
    At the center of the Star/Cross.

7.   At the center of the Star/Cross
     The teardrop
     Divides into many colors.
     There is
     A rainbow in the teardrop
     Where the sunlight
     Enters the forest
     And pierces the sorrows
     Of our life.

8.   Sitting on the stone in the clearing
     I see the circles of history,
     The endless repetitions of the past
     Moving before me;
     And I see a light
     That shines through pain
     Giving a sign of the future,
     Past and future meeting here
     At the center of the Star/Cross,
     A mystery
     And a message
     To be found
     In the Silence . . . In the Silence.

VIII

Breathing the Breath

of Mankind

Meditation Log   *Date*

1.   Holding myself in stillness
     I look into the open space
     At the center of the Star/Cross.
     It opens into infinity
     In each direction.
     The roots of the past are there
     And the unformed future.

2.   There is an energy
     Pulsating
     At the center of the Star/Cross.
     Strong,
     The beating of many hearts,
     Many lives
     Brought together
     In the course of the centuries,
     Layers of time
     Placed upon time
     To form the Star/Cross.
     The heartbeats of many lives
     Are in the Star/Cross.

3. The Star and the Cross are one,
    A unity
    Shaped by history.
    I stand before it
    Addressing it
    With my mind and heart
    Wondering at its message,
    Wondering what it means
    To meet a Star/Cross
    In the forest of one's life.

4. I seek my answers
    At the center of the Star/Cross,
    The place of Inward Visioning.
    In time past
    Inward Visioning
    Has been the way of peace,
    The path of the prophets of old.
    Now the place of Inward Visioning
    Is the center of the Star/Cross.
    The gate to peace opens
    At the center of the Star/Cross.

Meditation Log   *Date*

---

5. I look again
    Into the open space
    At the center of the Star/Cross.
    I am drawn into it.
    My body remains where it is,
    But my inner being is placed
    At the center of the Star/Cross.
    Past and future
    Are moving through me
    At the center of the Star/Cross.

6. My life is here
    At the center of the Star/Cross.
    I feel the past days of my life
    Come together as one day.
    I go over them in my mind.
    They are many days
    Filled with many things,
    But I feel them now
    As one day.
    I have been doing one thing,
    Becoming one life.
    Doing many things,
    I have been doing one thing,
    Becoming one life.

Meditation Log   *Date*

7.   At the center of the Star/Cross
     Time is moving through.
     All of time
     Is one moment,
     All of my life
     Is one moment,
     All of mankind's life
     Is one moment,
     So much behind,
     So much ahead,
     And all here
     Now,
     Moving through.
     Moving through
     This one point
     Where I am,
     Where mankind is.

Meditation Log   *Date*

8.   My life is here
     At the center of the Star/Cross
     With everyone's life.
     Carried on this one breath,
     Mankind and I
     Together
     As one.

9.   Breathing this one breath,
     Myself
     With everyone,
     Breathing my breath
     And the breath of everyone,
     Breathing the breath of mankind,
     Being in the open space
     At the center of the Star/Cross.

Meditation Log   *Date*

10. Being in the open space,
    Breathing the breath of mankind.
    Being my life,
    The life of mankind within me.
    Breathing,
    Being,
    Living my life,
    The life of mankind within me,
    At the center of the Star/Cross
    In the Silence . . . In the Silence.

About the Author

Dr. Ira Progoff has long been in the vanguard of those who have worked toward a dynamic psychology of creative and spiritual experience. In his practice as therapist, in his books, as lecturer and workshop leader, as Bollingen Fellow, and as Director of the Institute for Research in Depth Psychology at the Graduate School of Drew University, he has conducted pioneer research and developed new techniques that are widely used.

The core of Ira Progoff's theoretical work is contained in a trilogy of basic books. *The Death and Rebirth of Psychology* (1956) crystallizes the cumulative results of the work of the great historical figures in depth psychology and sets the foundation for a new psychology of personal growth. *Depth Psychology and Modern Man* (1959) presents the evolutionary perspective and formulates the basic concepts of Holistic Depth Psychology. *The Symbolic and the Real* (1963) pursues the philosophical implications of these ideas and applies them in developing new techniques for personal growth.

Proceeding from the Holistic Depth Psychology which he had developed, Dr. Progoff then created the *Intensive Journal* concept and process in 1966, publishing *At a Journal Workshop* as the basic text for its use in 1975. He first evolved the concept and method of Process Meditation in 1971 as a means of fulfilling the *Intensive Journal* process. After years of testing and development, it is now described in *The Practice of Process Meditation: The* INTENSIVE JOURNAL *Way to Spiritual Experience* (1980).

Dr. Progoff is Director of Dialogue House which, from its New York headquarters, administers the national and international outreach of the *Intensive Journal* program including Process Meditation.